SPOT

COMMUNITY HELPERS

DOCTORS

by Golriz Golkar

amicus LEARNING

throat

heart

Look for these words and pictures as you read.

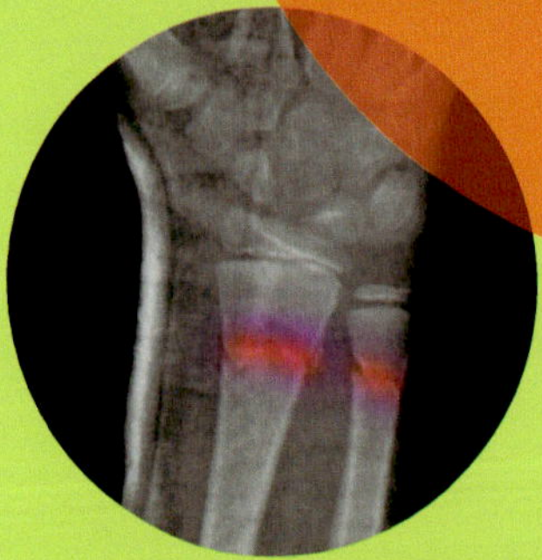

X-ray

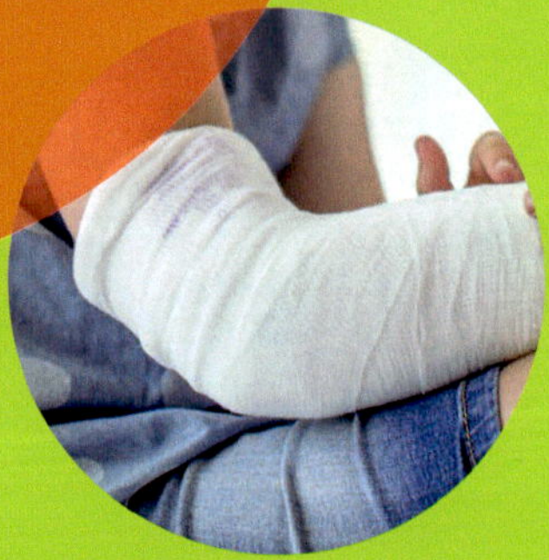

cast

Doctors are good helpers.
What do they do?

throat

Eve is at a checkup.

The doctor checks her throat.

Say ahh!

heart

The doctor listens to Leo's heart.

Take a deep breath.

Ba-dum. Ba-dum.

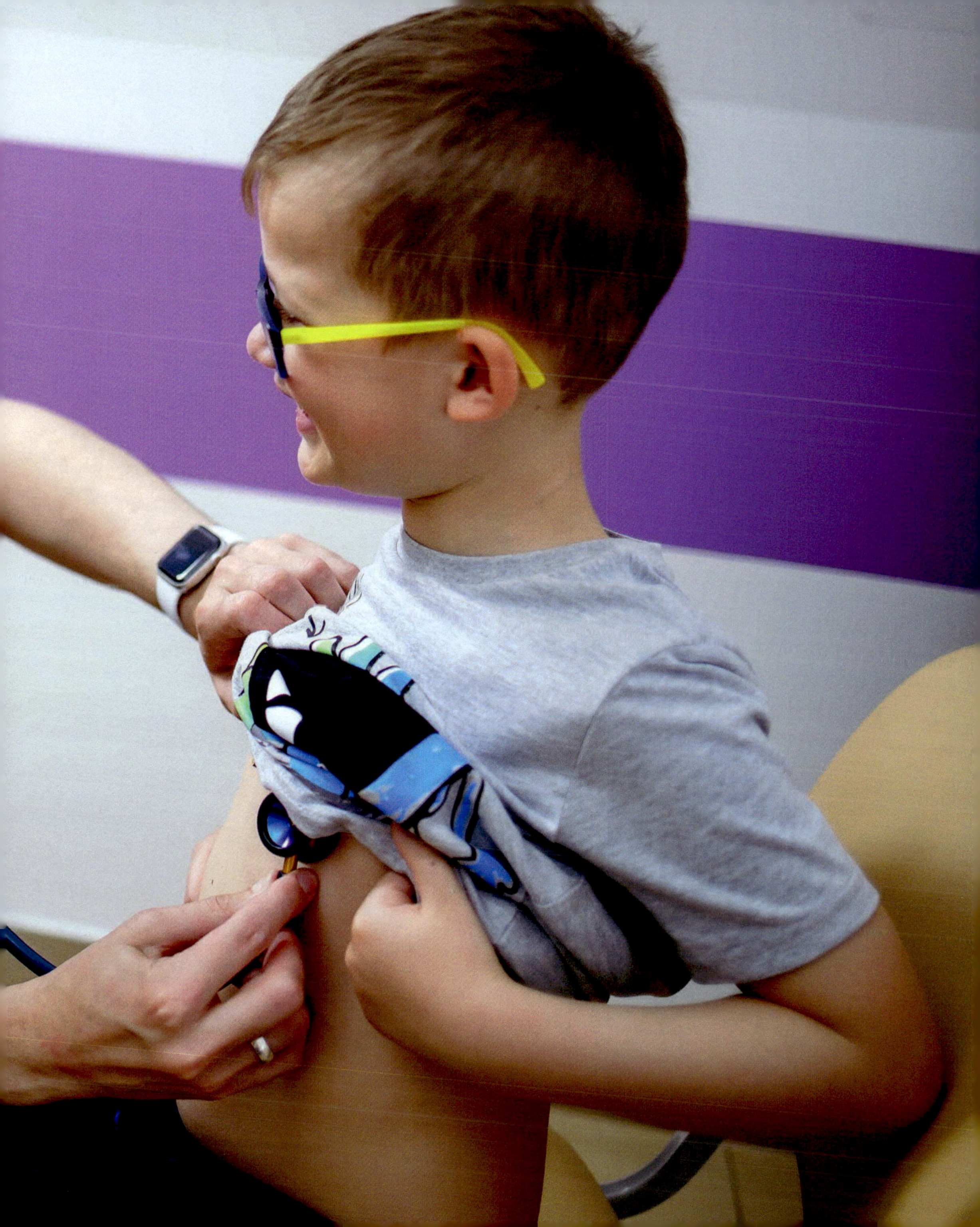

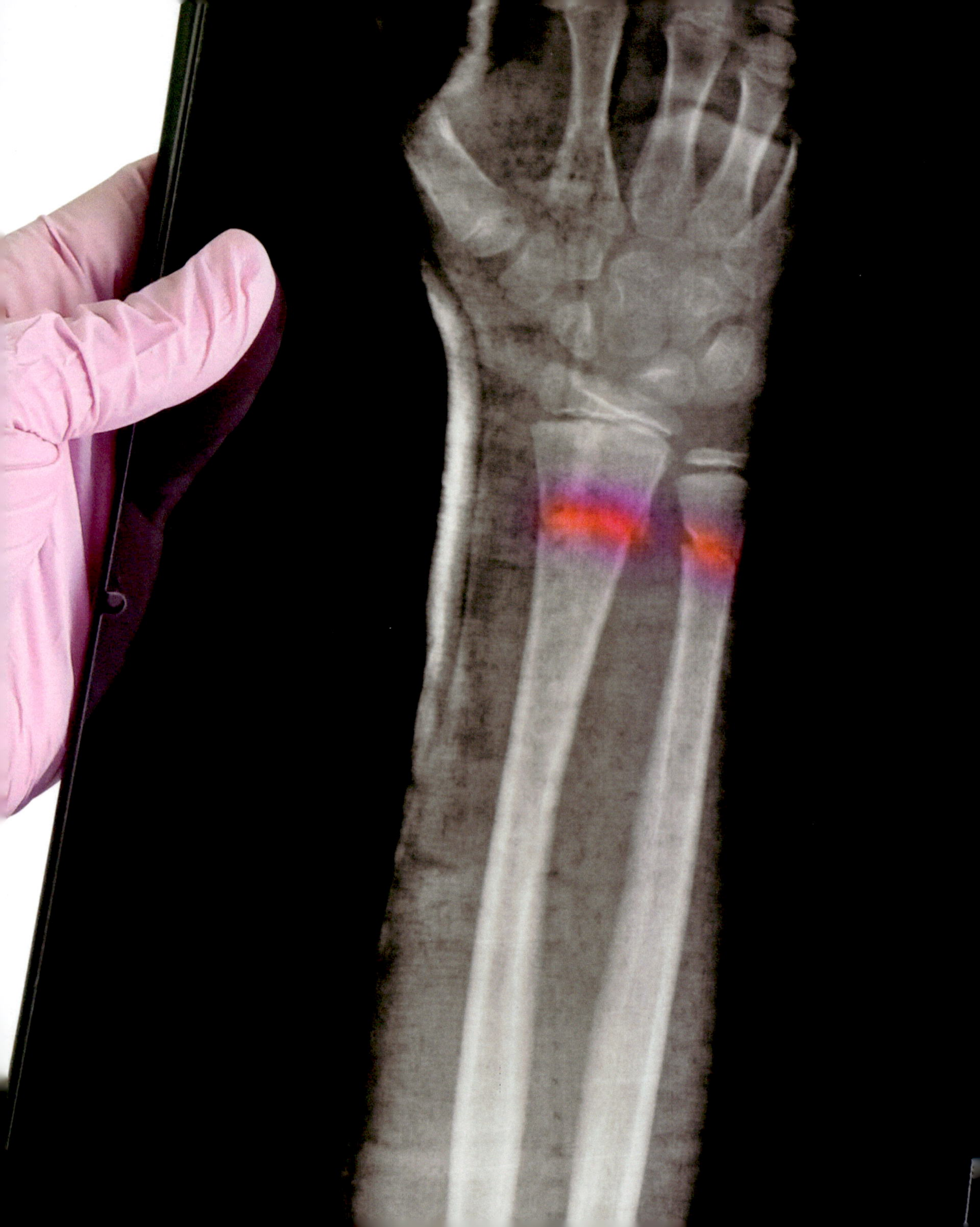

Is Rue's bone broken?

Hold still!

It is time for an X-ray.

X-ray

cast

Oh no!

Rue broke her arm.

The doctor puts on a cast.

Beep! Beep!
Ian's head is warm.
He needs some medicine.

Doctors help when we are sick.
They make us feel better!

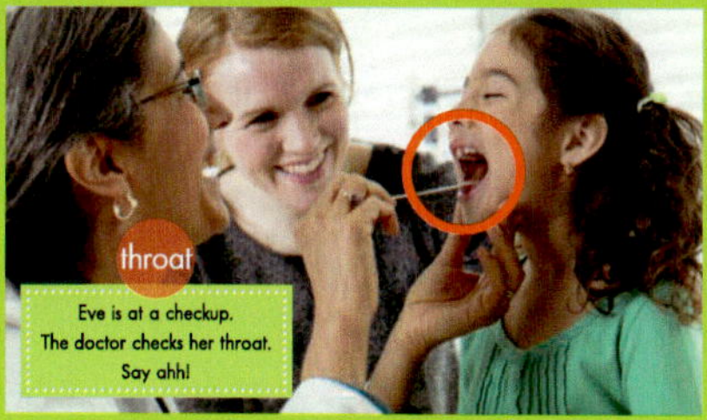

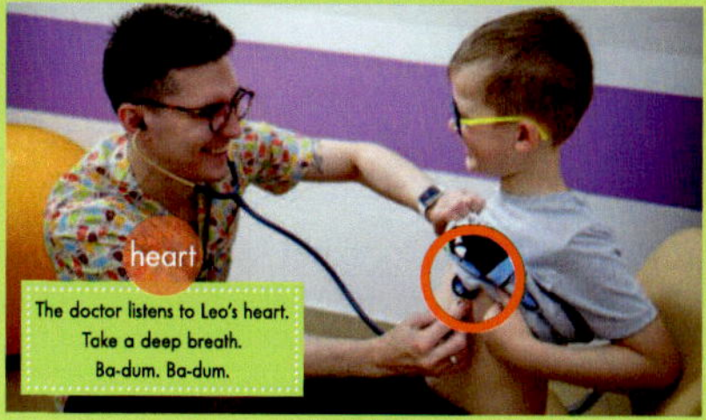

throat

heart

Did you find?

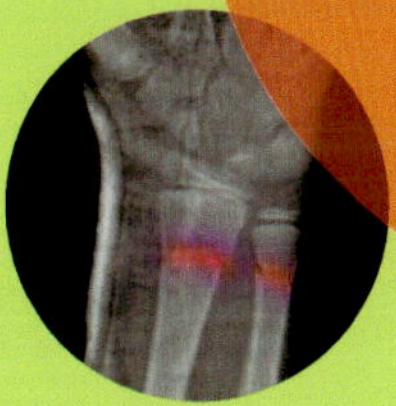

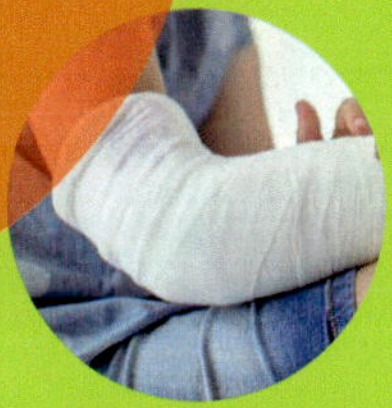

X-ray

cast

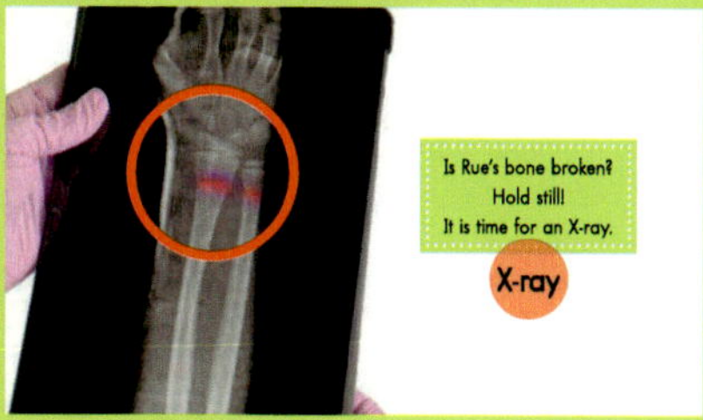

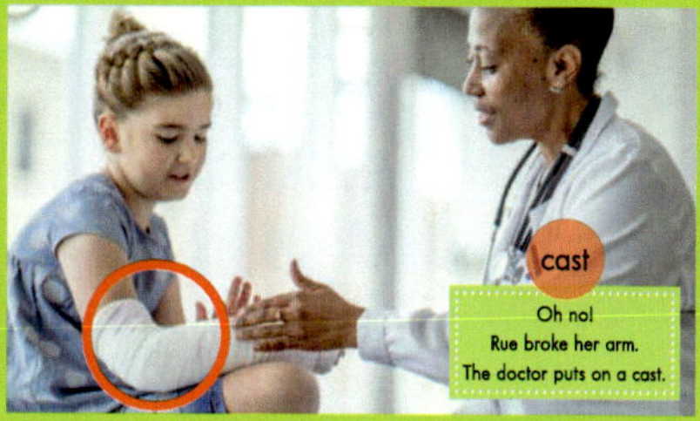

Spot is published by Amicus Learning, an imprint of Amicus
P.O. Box 227, Mankato, MN 56002
www.amicuspublishing.us

Library of Congress Cataloging-in-Publication Data
Names: Golkar, Golriz, author.
Title: Doctors / by Golriz Golkar.
Description: Mankato, MN : Amicus Learning, an imprint of Amicus, [2026] | Series: Spot community helpers | Audience: Ages 4–7 | Audience: Grades K–1 | Summary: "Doctors keep us healthy and happy. Learn how they help the community in this low-level beginning reader that reinforces new vocabulary with a search-and-find feature. A great early social studies book that will inspire kindergartners and first graders to learn about jobs in their community"— Provided by publisher.
Identifiers: LCCN 2024043703 (print) | LCCN 2024043704 (ebook) | ISBN 9798892004886 (library binding) | ISBN 9798892005425 (paperback) | ISBN 9798892005968 (ebook)
Subjects: LCSH: Physicians—Juvenile literature. | Medicine—Juvenile literature.
Classification: LCC R690 .G655 2026 (print) | LCC R690 (ebook) | DDC 610.69/5—dc23/eng/20241220
LC record available at https://lccn.loc.gov/2024043703
LC ebook record available at https://lccn.loc.gov/2024043704

Ana Brauer, editor
Deb Miner, series designer
Sara Hood, book designer and photo researcher

Photos by Getty Images/Callista Images, 8, FatCamera, 10–11, KidStock, 4-5, Maskot, 12–13; Shutterstock/ASDF_MEDIA, 1, Creativa Images, cover, DS Tkachuk, 6–7, LightField Studios, 3, NMK-Studio, 8, Spotmatik Ltd, 14